For they are my friends

For they are my friends

Photographs by Tom Marotta

Text by Mihail Eminescu (1850-1879),
and other Romanian sources.

With an introduction by Bob Adelman
and a foreword by W. D. Snodgrass.

Excerpts from *The Last Romantic: Mihail Eminescu,* which appear
throughout this book, copyright 1972 by UNESCO, were reprinted by
permission of the University Of Iowa Press.

ArtReflections, Inc.
Publisher
P.O. Box 935, Ansonia Station
New York, N.Y. 10023

Library of Congress Catalog Card
Number 76-43510
ISBN 0-917806-00-X
ISBN 0-917806-01-8

Printed in the U.S.A. by
Morgan Press, Inc.
Dobbs Ferry, N.Y.

ArtReflections, Inc. is a non-profit publisher dedicated to the art of photography.

To my dear Françoise, for her love,
devotion, patience and inspiration.

Acknowledgments

I want to thank all the people who participated in this book:

To *John Anelli* for his dedication and valuable assistance throughout this reportage.

For my father whose encouragement was my strength for so many years.

And to *Madeleine Popovici* for her love and understanding in helping to make a dream a reality.

I am most grateful for the cooperation and generous assistance to the following in providing material for this book:

Special thanks to *John E. Simmons,* director of the University Of Iowa Press, for allowing me to use quotations from Roy MacGregor-Hastie's *The Last Romantic: Mihail Eminescu.*

To the Romanian Library in New York for all their invaluable help.
The Office Of National Tourism, both in New York and in Romania.
The Photographic Society of Bucharest.
The Romanian Government and especially all our friends in Romania who allowed me to photograph them.

To *Zouzouka,* who spent many hours with us in preparation for our trip.

I am deeply indebted to *De* and *Camille Snodgrass* for all their assistance in helping me to put this book together.

I especially wish to thank *Carl Kravats* for helping me select these photographs as well as for his deep friendship.

Book design: Janet Solgaard

Typography: Examiner Graphics

Introduction

So the old country is still the same. Leafing through this portfolio, you might think you are looking at recently discovered turn-of-the-century photographs. Little clues tell us that they are contemporary— trucks out of focus, a blurred motocycle.

What Tom Marotta found were people enduring and enjoying the eternal peasant life. We see country people dressed in traditional garb, living amongst animals, doing handwork, finding simple pleasure in each other, and displaying raw grief at death.

The artifice and cunning of the photographer on page 37 permeates these pictures. Romania, I'm sure, has superhighways, factories, and modern cities, but that's everywhere and impersonal. The pictures look old-fashioned through some photographic sleight-of-hand. The photographer has chosen to select and isolate these people and their ways of life which seem for the moment to have been passed by, by time. In order to make intelligible the extraordinary photographs of the funeral, we have to see the old world of the mourners. Like Antonioni in China, he found peasant life with its slow rhythms and long traditions seemingly untouched by the socialist revolution. We know though that the other, the consumer revolution will catch them. Even now, I spotted tennis shoes and jeans. Soon there'll be supermarkets, portable radios and cars. Then the closed sanitary casket will arrive in a limo and we will have a sensible, rational funeral, rather than this primitive display of passion.

Bob Adelman

Foreword

Tom Marotta's photographs seem heavy with unfashionable virtues. You don't ask them the kind of question you ask pictures nowadays—matters of texture, composition, symbology. You ask them the questions you ask people. Marotta is most deeply concerned with his subjects; above all, the people he photographs. Yet he does not present those people for inspection; rather, he involves us in his relationship to them, their relation to him. One is caught up in the byplay of questioning and flirtation between subject and photographer. It is a little like waking up in the middle of a love affair whose history you have forgotten. These pictures, recording Marotta's affection for the people of Romania, carry the residues and resonances of earlier events and details in that relation. Eminescu's line aptly titles the book: *For They Are My Friends.*

Not that the picture's success depends on our knowing, or discovering, those details; one measure of the picture's success, though, is how much it makes us *want* to ask. Look at Plate 18, for instance—a delicious contrast between a line of gnarled and sprightly old men and a smooth and lovely young girl. Marotta found the men working near the monastery at Suceava; when he had them lined up, one said "Wait! Get the pretty girl!" and pulled Tom's wife, Francoise, into the line. Then, the young Romanian girl in charge of admissions to the monastery was persuaded to take her place. We needn't know this—what we must see is the proud elegance of that hand on the Pepsi bottle, the unquenchable gleam in those ancient eyes. In Plate 47 is a lady who ran up to Marotta in the village market, saying, "Wait; I'm an English teacher. I can translate for you!" What we need is to see the tremulous radiance in that tiny frame, the eagerness mixed with self-amused shyness in those wrinkled hands.

Not that it would hurt to have visited the black pottery workshops at Marginea or the rug weavers near Sapinta; yet Plates 27, 28 and 29 deliver us the essential serenity and fulfillment these people find in their work. Anyone with half an eye sees the boyish curiousity of Plate 12, the disastrously tucked-in shirt, the gawky, stork-like eagerness. We needn't know that Marotta had left his camera on a timed shutter-release and walked teasingly away, leaving the boys to peer in delight and anxiety at the ticking box: what will it do now?

Looking at Plate 61, we know this man has truly suffered; we also know he has long used that suffering as a weapon against the world. It matters little that he actually *was* begging in the park. We always knew he was a beggar in a deeper sense and our response has a strong mixture of distaste and pity.

Again, we see the incredible mother and son of Plate 46. Obviously, the woman is poor; we notice the safety pin replacing the buttons on her worn out sweater. Marotta, though, includes her among the scandalously rich: her smile tells everything about the self-confident richness of her life. On her chest two more safety pins glitter like a sheriff's badge or medals on a sergeant's jacket. She can manage. We see, too, the enormous depth of affection in her son's eyes and carriage.

Yet, for me at least, something paradoxical happens with more looking. Contrast the tough, cocky Gypsy boy in Plate 55: barefoot, hatted, one hand in pocket, one holding a cigarette. One's first impulse is pity—he seems so obviously a neglected child of the streets. But on second look, the values shift. Perhaps that *is* his mother behind him, looking beaten down, sickly. Here, it is the son who looks capable. The boy in the earlier picture scarcely looked at the world at all—at least, he looked at his mother, first. Is it possible that her self-confidence produces a hesitant, frightened child; or that her warmth and goodness provide something so valuable that he learns to care for little else?

Again, contrast the well-to-do child of Plate 11. Clearly, he has known advantages not open to the other two, and may have possibilities beyond them. Yet we find in him something cold, detached, spoiled, almost narcissistic. He has grown up in the spotlight—which often enough produces an effect like bleaching.

We are left asking the sort of question we ask about our friends. Of course one wants his own child to have ''advantages;'' is it possible they could be ''drawbacks?'' Like most works of art, Marotta's photographs cannot tell us how to live, cannot solve our dilemma; it is their mission to enrich it.

Still, of this life, one thing is unambiguously predictable: it will end. So far, I have neglected the book's real triumph, the climax to which it has carefully built—the funeral of a boy in his early 20's. Even here there are paradoxes, ironies: the funeral is held in the famous Gay Graveyard at Sapinta, whose grave-markers are composed, carved and painted by Ion Stan Patras. Every year thousands of tourists from all over the world visit this graveyard. How few of them—charmed by the brightly colored, decorated crosses, by Patras' candid, humorous, sarcastic, elegaic verses, by the charming scenes of village life he carves on the grave markers—how few think of the episodes of stark tragedy enacted there before those markers can be raised. It is this tragedy Marotta has preserved.

We follow the funeral from the procession through the village, to the actual lowering of the coffin; from the fresh little girls, snickering at the photographer, hands over their mouths, to the weeping faces of the friends and family, aging, clenched in grief, hands again over their mouths.

We see the young boy, emaciated, carried by his brother and friends, the sturdy young men his own age; we see his mother bending to kiss his face through the gravecloth as the coffin lid approaches from behind. We see the muscular arms of the men, the blessing arm of the priest, the pleading, expressive arms of the mourning women calling the boy from his grave, the compassionately linked arms that restrain them from the closing coffin. We are left with the faces of grief.

Yet the last word is not the only word. Nor the most important. Marotta shook for hours after taking these pictures. Well he might. It took a very special photographer, a very special people and a very special relationship between them for these pictures to be taken. Only a man they deeply trusted would be allowed such entry to their grief, their vulnerability. Only a people who deeply respected their own lives could feel honored when someone like Patras or Marotta records and preserves those lives, not as they would like to see them, but as they truly were.

W.D. Snodgrass

We revolve in this infinity, always forgetting
that this whole world is just an instant hovering in Time:

There where the Carpathians are, high crested,
there under the plane trees, on the hills, ranked like armies,
the mountains stand rigidly to attention under the blue sky.

And then the world was born, the moon, the sun, the elements . . .

Since then, till now, along unknown paths come colonies
of lost worlds, surging out of the dark valleys of chaos,
bursting forth, shining hosts, out of infinity . . .

They are drawn to life by a limitless desire to exist.
And we, children of the little world inside the universe
build anthills on our inconsiderable earth:

Generation follows generation and we think ourselves marvellous,

Near a low foothill
At Heaven's doorsill,
Where the trail's descending
To the plain and ending,
Here three shepherds keep
Their three flocks of sheep,

A king weaving for the world a century of plans
while the poor man thinks only of tomorrow . . .

Some, sated with pleasure, enjoy life
day after day divided only into hours of smiles.

Holy father, worthy priest,
Answer me one question, please:
A little wife that still looks good,
May she make love when she could?
A wife that's married to a man,
May she make love when she can?
"Both with me, and you also,
Only not a soul must know;
Both with me and with another
But her man must not discover,
Nor the town, she's got a lover;
Both with me and anyone,
With the priest from the next town—
That's forgiven soon, at least,
Since it's no sin with the priest."

In every man there is a world trying to get out,
Old Demiurge struggling still, but struggling in vain;
and in the mind of every man, the old question again:
where did it come from, where is it going
this flowering of desire sown in the void?

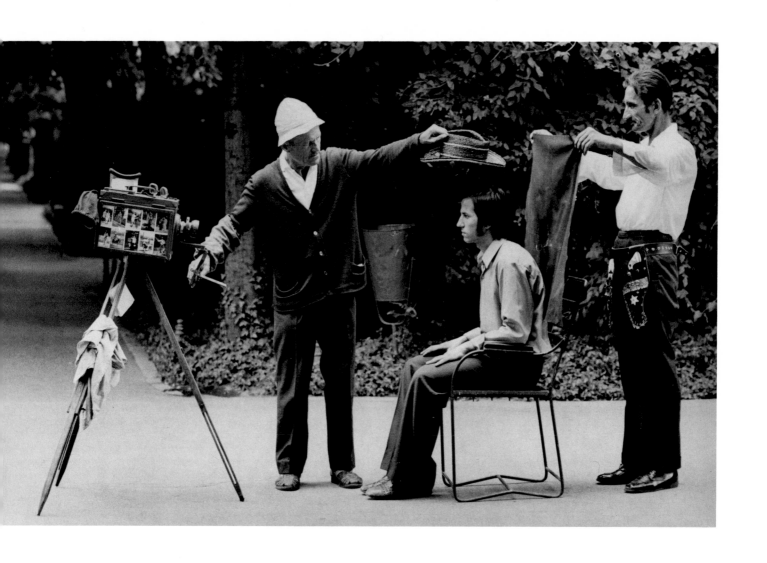

. . . his thoughts drag back into visibility
thousands of centuries past,

. . . but in an instant his thoughts can carry him
thousands of centuries into the future.

There are many women here on earth
whose eyes scatter sparks . . .
not even the highest born are worth
as much as you, as much as you.

If one only knew . . . How many white hands had gathered those perfumed flowers.

A single man is in them all, one thing alone in everything.
He who can rises above the others, and they
in the shadows with a humble heart, forgotten,
lose themselves secretly like unseen spray.
Blind fate takes no notice of their thoughts, of their desires . . .

. . . What have they seen?
How much could they tell us if only they had a voice?

. . . let the gentle stars give back brightness
to her eyes and
let the old moon shine down to wake again
her golden hair .

I've only one wish left—
that they'll let me die
in the quiet of the evening
by some seaside

Let no one stand and weep,
. . . let there be just one sound,
. . . Let the sound of the herd bell
cut the evening breeze,

. . . and the gruff voice of the sea
then will moan
full of passion, but I will be
dust, and alone.

65

The Merry Cemetery of Sapinta

If the ceremony of wedding has always been a symbol of ageless youth, of ceaseless life on earth, the rites and ceremonies of burial have sanctioned the Romanian people's attitude towards death.

The tradition of watching the dead, of preparing the funeral feasts combines with laments and ancient ceremonial psalm readings, wherein the deceased man's life, the grief of the relatives and acquaintances, are recalled.

In villages of northern Moldavia and northern Oltenia, as well as Banat, they bring fir-tree branches which are put on the graves of young, unmarried people as a symbol of youth and of the deeds they should have achieved during their lifetime.

Carved posts, of unequalled beauty and artistic value, are stuck by the grave of the dead. Sometimes these signs bear inscriptions and drawings, and along with the artistic accomplishments of the folk artist, one can also perceive something of the Romanian's attitude towards life and death.

There is a graveyard in Sapinta, Maramures, with wood cut posts carved by Ion Stan Patras, which came to be known throughout the world as the "Merry Cemetery of Sapinta", owing to the caustic lines and drawings which recall scenes and features of him who died.

Death as well as life is a combination between joy and youth, optimism and wise acceptance of the natural flow of man's life.

Author's note

The son of Pop Ioan had died, in his early youth, two days before our arrival in Sapinta. On the following pages is a reportage which depicts the ceremony of burial in the Merry Cemetery of Sapinta. Before photographing the funeral I had asked permission to photograph the ceremony from the deceased boy's mother and she said she would be honored.

This series of photographs is one of the most touching reportages I have ever done and the memory of that day will remain forever vivid in my mind.

In the fields the cuckoo sung
Telling me I would die young
I went boying through this earth
Shorter than a life is worth
Death came hurrying pretty early
Just when we loved earth most dearly
Wicked death with ugly name
When I was so young you came
Since you seized us at no more
Than the age of 24.

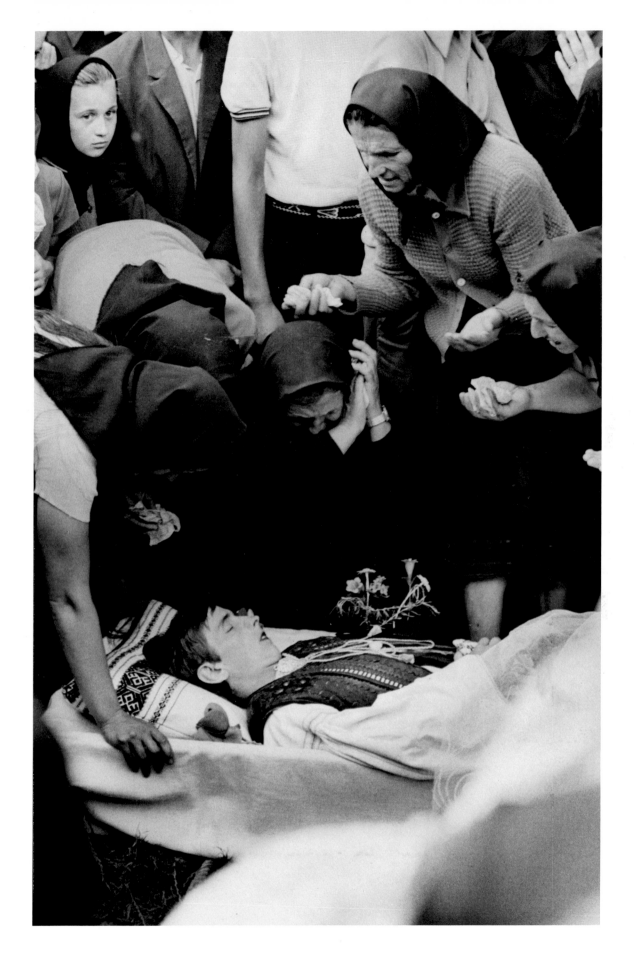

SOMNOROASE PĂSĂRELE . . . .

Now the songbirds, all adrowse,
Come together out of sight
In their nests among the boughs—
       So; goodnight.

Only small springs go on weeping
While the dark woods hush and cease;
Even the garden flowers are sleeping—
       Sleep, then, in peace.

Across the water, the swan's gliding
Toward the reeds that guard his nest;
Angels 'round you still abiding,
       Calm be your rest.

Now over night's broad elfery
The ancient, proud moon claims her height.
All is peace, all harmony;
       Now, goodnight.

LIST OF PLATES—PHOTOGRAPHY

LIST OF PLATES—POETRY